THE
FACTS
ABOUT

LATCHKEY
CHILDREN

BY
Judy Monroe

EDITED BY
Anita Larsen

CONSULTANT
Elaine Wynne, M.A., Licensed Psychologist

CRESTWOOD HOUSE
New York

CIP

LIBRARY OF CONGRESS CATALOGING IN PUBLICATION DATA

Monroe, Judy
  Latchkey Children

  (The facts about)
  Includes index.
  SUMMARY: Discusses various aspects of the lives of latchkey children, such as why they must come home to an empty house, how they interact with brothers and sisters, how they can use the telephone to find help in emergency situations, and how they spend their time alone.
  1. Latchkey children — United States — Juvenile literature. [1. Latchkey children.] I. Larsen, Anita. II. Title. III. Series.
HQ777.65.M65   1989   306.874—dc20   89-1383
ISBN 0-89686-438-3

PHOTO CREDITS

Cover: DRK Photo: Don & Pat Valenti
Berg & Associates: (Arnold J. Kaplan) 4, 10, 41; (Margaret C.
  Berg) 17; (Dick Wade) 18; (Bob Higbee) 25; (Kirk Schlea) 28
DRK Photo: (Don & Pat Valenti) 9, 15, 30, 35
FPG International: (Michael A. Keller) 36
Journalism Services: (Dennis W. Trowbridge) 42

CRESTWOOD HOUSE

Macmillan Publishing Company
866 Third Avenue
New York, NY 10022
Collier Macmillan Canada, Inc.

Produced by Carnival Enterprises
Printed in the United States of America
First Edition
10 9 8 7 6 5 4 3 2 1

TABLE OF CONTENTS

TONY AND SUSIE

It's 3:15 P.M. School is out. Tony, age eleven, heads for home. He stops at his front door. Sliding out his key, he opens the door. Once inside, he locks the door, then checks through the house. As usual, no one is home. Everything is quiet.

Tony flips on the TV. Later, he makes a peanut butter and banana sandwich. He eats it with a big glass of milk. After rinsing off his dirty dishes, he begins his math homework.

Tony's mother gets home three hours later. Tony smiles when he sees her. He knows she worries about him staying by himself.

But Tony knows she has no choice. His mother does not earn enough money to hire a baby-sitter. And Tony wants to take care of himself after school. He has agreed to follow his mother's rules when he is home alone.

Tony is a *latchkey child*. He is regularly alone for a period of time during the day. Tony spends about three hours by himself after school.

Twelve-year-old Susie, too, is a latchkey child. Her father is at home when she returns after school. But each morning, Susie gets herself up at 5:30 A.M. Her father has already gone to work. She dresses, then fixes three lunches. "Get up, sleepyheads!" she calls to her two younger sisters. Once they are out of bed, Susie helps them dress. She makes sure they each eat a bowl of cold cereal and milk. Susie walks the two little girls to their *day-care center*, then goes on to her own school.

Tony and Susie are used to taking care of themselves for a few hours. But many people still have questions about latchkey children. How many latchkey children are there? Can they care for themselves properly? Where did the term *latchkey children* come from?

WHAT DOES "LATCHKEY CHILDREN" MEAN?

In the early 1800s, few American children were left alone for long. Most families lived on farms, and working parents were usually close by. Grandparents and aunts also helped care for children.

But some children had no one at home to greet them after school. Their parents were working, often on jobs in a nearby town or city. To get into their homes, these children had to lift the latches or fasteners on their front doors.

By the early 1900s, more families had moved from farms to towns and cities. During this period, latchkey children were called *dorks*—for the door keys they used to get into their empty houses. The word *dork* soon faded from use.

But when teachers began seeing children wearing

6

house keys tied to strong strings hung around their necks, they began to use the term *latchkey children*.

Today, there are many latchkey arrangements. Some latchkey children care for themselves. Others go to day-care centers. Still others stay with relatives or neighbors they know or baby-sitters, nannies, or housekeepers their families have hired. There are also those who go to school activities, clubs, or classes by themselves.

HOW MANY LATCHKEY CHILDREN ARE THERE?

The number of latchkey children in America grew quickly in the 1940s. Many fathers left home to fight in World War II and a lot of mothers went to work to earn money for their families.

When the men returned, quite a few women kept their jobs. By 1947, one out of five mothers worked outside the home. Four years later, one out of three mothers had a job. As a result, the number of latchkey children climbed during the late 1940s and early 1950s.

The number of latchkey children grew for other reasons, too. America was changing. *One-parent homes* were more common. Divorces increased. Families continued to move to bigger cities, but grandparents and aunts did not necessarily move with them. So grandparents and aunts were not there to watch the children.

Many families could not afford baby-sitters. Day-care centers were not yet available.

The *baby boom* between 1946 and 1958 added to the numbers of latchkey children. Births increased and more and more mothers held jobs outside the home. By 1987, 60 percent of women with children (about 9 million) were working outside their homes. Many of them were single parents who could not pay for day care, baby-sitters, or live-in help for their children. Many two-parent families could not afford this help either.

In 1976, there were 1.6 million latchkey children in the United States (13 percent of all American children). By 1987, 7 million children cared for themselves before or after school (24 percent). Experts do not think there will be fewer latchkey children in the future. The number of one-parent homes is increasing along with the number of working mothers. So the number of children left on their own will probably increase, too.

STORIES

Ever since latchkey children have been around, stories about them have grown. These false ideas make some children ashamed to admit they are latchkey children.

One story is that their parents *neglect* them. There is no proof of this. Most parents think *self-care* is a good choice. They train their children to take care of themselves and stay in close touch by phone.

Seven million children cared for themselves before or after school in 1987. Many experts expect this number to increase.

Another story is that latchkey children get low grades in school. This is not true. Studies by school officials show that latchkey children get the same grades or even better grades than other children.

One dangerous story is that latchkey children have low *self-esteem*. Not true! In fact, many children enjoy being by themselves. They like time alone. They do not have problems talking with their friends, other children, or adults. Joseph is an example of a latchkey child with high self-esteem.

"I've taken care of myself after school for two

years," said Joseph, age fourteen. "I like the freedom to do what I want in the afternoons. I'm on the school football and softball teams. And when I come home from school, I do a few chores, then my homework."

Some children do have problems with self-care, of course. But it is a good choice for responsible and independent children like Joseph.

NO ONE IS HOME

Between two and three o'clock in the afternoon, millions of school bells sound across the United States. Children pour out of school, but about a quarter of them do not go home to waiting parents.

Joan is one of them. She lets herself into her house each day. Joan is ten and has been a latchkey child for two years. She calls her mother right away, then walks her dog, Lucky, around the block. Joan likes to have the TV on while she does her homework. At 6 P.M., she sets the table. She watches from the big living room window for her mother. When school is closed or if she is sick, Joan stays home alone. During the summer, Joan and Lucky live with Aunt Shirley.

Many latchkey children, like Joan, spend their afternoons alone. Joan has no *siblings* (brothers and sisters). Joan's mother thought her daughter would be all right alone for three hours each afternoon. Her mother explains, "Joan is quiet and responsible. She follows my

Many latchkey children have a regular after-school routine. They get home, call their mom or dad, make a snack, and do their homework.

rules. For instance, I know she doesn't have her friends over when I'm not home."

Researchers agree there is no best age to start self-care. One study showed that many parents believe children can care for themselves by the time they're in third grade. Others think that children are generally not ready for self-care until they are twelve.

The amount of time latchkey children spend alone also differs. Like Joan, many latchkey children are alone for two or three hours after school before their parents come home from work. But some children, like Dave, spend five or more hours alone.

Dave is twelve. His divorced mother is a nurse. She works from 3:00 P.M. to 11:00 P.M., Monday through Friday. Dave spends all evening by himself. He cooks his own meals and does the dishes and some chores. After homework and TV, he gets himself to bed. He sees his mother only in the mornings and on weekends.

Most latchkey children, however, expect to have one parent home between 5 and 6 P.M. at night. Occasionally, parents may not get home on time because they work overtime. Accidents, snarled traffic, and car problems also cause delays. Sometimes parents buy groceries or gas after work. This extra time before parents arrive home often causes latchkey children needless worry. They imagine something bad has happened unless parents call to say they are going to be late and what time they'll be home. That is how Stephanie and her father manage it.

"Dad is home by five," said Stephanie, age thirteen. "But he sometimes works late. Then he calls and tells me he won't be home until seven or so. So I make myself a sandwich and wait."

Some parents don't give their children any *guidelines* or rules. Other parents don't say more than "Behave," "Do your homework," or "Stay out of trouble." One eight-year-old boy was told, "Lock the door and don't play with matches." In these cases, children have to make up their own rules.

Most parents do give their children firm rules, though. John's parents made this list:

1. Lock the door.
2. Call us the minute you get home.
3. Don't let anyone in.
4. Don't tell anyone you are alone.
5. If someone asks for your parents, say, "They are busy and will call back later."
6. Don't cook.
7. In an emergency, call one of us right away.

Other parents have similar rules, which their children usually follow, along with their own familiar, daily routines. For example, after calling their parents, many children watch TV. Having TV voices and laughter in the house makes it seem less empty.

Since many latchkey children watch TV for four or five hours a day, some parents have rules for that, too.

"My parents said I can watch TV after I finish my homework," said Tricia. "But I do my homework while I watch TV."

Like Tricia's mom and dad, many parents ask their children to finish their homework before watching TV. Some tell their children not to watch certain programs like the news. But it's hard for parents to enforce these rules. "My parents tell me not to watch programs that say 'parental guidance suggested,'" said a ten-year-old girl. "I watch them anyway. Then I get scared." Other children stick to the rules. "My parents and I agreed which shows I can watch," said Shelly, age twelve. "Then I can talk with my parents about the shows when they get home."

While some latchkey children have no chores to do after school, many do. They might sweep, dust, clean the bathroom, make beds, set the table, empty the trash, or vacuum. They change chores from time to time to keep from getting bored with the same old things.

Parents often have rules about playing outdoors. Many insist that their children stay indoors. The younger the child, the more this is true.

"I have to stay inside after school," said Bob, age ten. "I wish I could play outdoors. My friends are playing baseball." By the fourth or fifth grade, some latchkey children are allowed to play outside. Usually, they must first ask their parents.

Latchkey children may also play less with friends indoors. Absent parents worry about accidents and fights. So latchkey children usually can't have friends over or go to a friend's home unless an adult is there. In fact, not being able to see friends is a common complaint.

Because of these rules, one out of every three latchkey children spends an afternoon alone except for TV and telephone calls.

BROTHERS AND SISTERS

"After school, my sister, Kathy, and I watch TV. We also talk about school, clothes, and maybe play a

After school, many latchkey children have certain chores to do each day. Brothers and sisters usually help each other complete the tasks.

game," said Wendy. "But sometimes we fight."

Fighting is the most common problem between latch-key siblings. They fight over big and little things, often because they're angry. Even though they understand their parents have good reasons for being away, sometimes coping makes them mad. Parents try to reduce the chance of fights breaking out by setting rules. For example, siblings get along best if they have their own chores to do.

"My older brother and I have our own chores to do after school," explained Frank, age nine. "Then we do homework. I know my brother is in charge. So I have to listen to him." A fourteen-year-old girl said, "I'm not to correct my little brother. My parents do that when they come home."

When fights break out, some children call their parents for help. Others learn to settle disputes themselves. Sometimes, siblings wait for a parent to come home, then let the parent settle the fight.

Younger children often think they are controlled by their older siblings. "John is bossy," said seven-year-old Pat. "He won't let me watch cartoons. We have to watch his favorite TV shows. And he eats more than his half of the treats. I wish I was the oldest!"

When there are two or more children, the oldest is usually in charge. He or she often holds the house key. When everyone is safely at home, he or she calls the parent. As a rule, the oldest helps with homework, settles fights, watches siblings playing outside, and deals with emergencies.

Older siblings do not always like this responsibility. They may not have enough time for themselves. They can't see friends after school, and they may be too busy watching their younger siblings to finish their own homework. They often worry that their younger siblings will hurt themselves or the house. Then they'll get blamed and be punished.

Fights are more common among *stepbrothers* and *stepsisters*. When two families merge, the children may feel angry and jealous. Stepsiblings might not want to

Older siblings are sometimes bossy. Younger siblings sometimes don't listen to directions. Brothers and sisters must learn to work together when their parents are not around.

share their mom or dad with their new siblings. There may also be a change in family position.

Jamie was the oldest child, but after his mother's remarriage, his stepsister, Linda, was the oldest. Now she is in charge after school. When the two fight, Jamie tells Linda, "You're not my sister. I don't have to do what you say."

Preparing siblings for self-care is harder than preparing a single child to stay alone. Parents need to work with each child. Brothers and sisters should know how to care for one another. Each child should be able to handle emergencies. Everyone should agree to and know the rules for snacks, TV, chores, and other problem situations. And each sibling should understand that he or she is part of the self-care team.

FEARS AND WORRIES

Latchkey children sometimes feel afraid when no grown-up is around. They worry about break-ins and being hurt by strangers. They are concerned that fights with siblings may result in damage to their houses or to each other.

The worst fear is of a robbery, however. Latchkey children are occasionally frightened when they hear an animal crying or barking. They think someone is trying to break into their homes. Eleven-year-old Will said, "When I hear a strange noise, I worry that someone is breaking into the house. Then I'll get hurt."

When no grown-up is around, latchkey children may feel afraid.

Fearfulness does tend to be more common among latchkey children. Feelings of fear also last longer for latchkey children. They have no adults to comfort them or to explain what the strange noises are. They must wait a long time before parents come home to talk with them.

Ten-year-old Jenny thinks she hears noises in her basement. "The noises come once a week," she said. "I get scared. So I lock myself in the bathroom and wait for my dad. He gets home by five-thirty each night." Jenny will not tell her parents about her fears. She wants to take care of herself.

Children who are alone and afraid handle their fears in different ways. Some hide in places they think are safe, like bathrooms, showers, under beds, or in closets. If they are small enough, some children climb into bathroom or kitchen cabinets. Other children turn up the volume on the TV or radio to drown out strange noises. Some children check their houses when they first come home. "I look under the beds, in the closets, and behind the doors," explained Chris. "I do this every day."

Some latchkey children call their parents when something frightens them, but won't tell their parents about their fears. "Staying alone is what my parents and I decided," said Rich, age eleven. "If I tell them I'm afraid, it would make them feel bad."

Researchers find that being bored is also a problem for latchkey children. Boredom increases both fear and sibling fights. A busy child is less likely to argue with siblings or hear noises. But some children find it hard to plan activities and to organize their time after school. "It's boring at home," Bonnie said, age eleven. "There isn't anything to do after school except TV."

Many latchkey children overcome boredom by doing things from lists they and their parents worked on together. Some play games, read, watch TV, call friends, write to pen pals, work on hobbies, do homework, exercise, or listen to music.

Pets are great, too. Dogs and cats increase feelings of safety and comfort. Playing with pets and caring for them can make the house feel less empty.

Even when they aren't bored or fearful, some children in self-care feel lonely. They usually miss their parents after school, and nearly all complain that they cannot see their friends.

THE PHONE LINK

A telephone can go a long way toward easing a child's loneliness. Both parents and children feel better when they can call to "check in."

Eleven-year-old Bruce said, "My mom or dad calls me at four each afternoon. They ask how school went and tell me not to watch too much TV. They usually talk a few minutes. But that means a lot to me."

Many latchkey children like to call their parents during the afternoon to check in or to share daily news. Or they might have questions: "What can I have for a snack?" "Can I play outdoors?" "Can I have friends over?" Some children call parents for homework help.

The telephone can also be the solution to an emergency. Once when he was eleven, Jim went into the kitchen to make popcorn for himself and his younger brothers. As Jim started to heat oil in a pan, a fight broke out between his brothers. He rushed to the living room. After settling the quarrel, he remembered his popcorn. But he couldn't get into the kitchen—the oil had caught on fire! Smoke poured out.

Jim grabbed the phone in the living room. He dialed 911 and reported the fire. Then he dragged his brothers outside and shut the front door behind him. The fire trucks came in less than five minutes.

Because Jim acted quickly, little was harmed. The burnt pan was thrown away. The only damage was that the house smelled smokey for a few days. Jim's parents had taught him how and when to call 911. The family had practiced fire drills, so Jim knew how to get himself and his brothers out. He also remembered to close the door behind him when he saw fire. Jim knew a fire grows if it has fresh air.

DANGERS AND SOLUTIONS

A telephone call can connect a latchkey child to a parent and can summon help. But it can bring danger, too. So some parents instruct their children to answer only arranged telephone signals. "When I hear the phone ring two times, I know it's my mom," said a fourteen-year-old boy. Other families use telephone answering machines to screen calls. Latchkey children pick up phones only when they hear familiar voices over the answering machines.

Telephone safety is an important concern for latchkey children. How would you have handled Ruth's situation? Thirteen-year-old Ruth had just gotten home from school. The phone rang. She picked it up, thinking it was her dad. Instead, she heard a strange man's voice. He said he was going to climb into her apartment that night. "I didn't know his voice," she remembered. "I didn't say anything. I just hung up right away."

The phone rang again. Ruth moved into the kitchen. The phone rang and rang, but she didn't answer it. When the ringing stopped, she called her dad at work to tell him what had happened. Ruth's father called a neighbor and arranged for his daughter to stay there after school for the rest of the week. Ruth didn't get any more calls.

Ruth and her dad later talked to the police. They learned that obscene and threatening phone calls seldom occur. The best way to handle them is to do exactly what Ruth did—hang up right away.

Other dangers that latchkey children face are injuries, fires, and traffic accidents. You've already read how Jim handled the danger of fire by calling 911 when his popcorn oil blazed up. Electrical appliances, toasters, and stoves can also cause fires. So can any clothing, potholders, curtains, or paper near them.

Injuries like ten-year-old Tanya's are also important to consider. Tanya was playing near her garage. Her dad had recently had a new roof put on it. She stepped on a rusty nail and her foot began to bleed. She called her dad, but he was in a meeting.

Tanya's solution was to wait two hours before her dad came home and drove her to the hospital. She had no other adult to go to for help. She did not know how to call for an ambulance or rescue squad.

How would you handle it?

When they're injured, most latchkey children do wait for their parents to return home. Some, like Tanya, call their parents for help. This isn't always the best solution. It's often better to know when an emergency exists and how to call an emergency number and ask for help. Then try to relax. The emergency service will usually arrive before a parent can. It can be helpful to call a nearby adult, too. Sometimes, it's better to wait and call the parents when the emergency is over and everyone is safe.

It's a good idea to be able to handle minor injuries at

24 *Parents should teach their children first aid. That way, if the parents are at work, kids can handle small cuts, bruises, and bug bites themselves.*

home, too. Injuries include animal bites, burns, cuts and scrapes, insect stings, nosebleeds, and poisonings. If children have first aid kits and know how to use them, they can take care of some of these injuries themselves.

What's in a good first aid kit? It might include different sizes of bandages, gauze pads, tape, scissors, tweezers, cotton balls, a thermometer, aspirin (or similar medicine), and an icepack. Children can practice applying calamine lotion or baking soda to take the sting out of insect bites. It's easy to put on a little iodine or peroxide to clean cuts.

Traffic accidents can happen when children walk to and from school or play outside. It's scary being in a traffic accident, even if no one is hurt. But there are steps you can take to help out. The first is to report the accident to the police—right away. The second is to answer the police officers' questions. The police question everyone, so no child should feel singled out. Children often feel they have been careless if they were in a traffic accident. But this is not necessarily the case. Drivers cause accidents, as well.

The key to home safety is being prepared. Unexpected things can happen. Children should know what to do if water pipes freeze, or if there is a storm.

In addition to a first aid kit, families can put together a severe weather kit. Such a kit might include a portable radio, a flashlight, batteries, no-cook food, bottled water, and a first aid kit.

In case of emergencies, latchkey children should also know directions to their homes, as well as their telephone numbers and addresses. Children and parents can agree on people in the neighborhood who will help. And it's a good idea to run through emergency drills!

SICK DAYS

"Mom, I have a stomachache. Can I stay home from school?" asked Steve, age ten.

"No," said his mom, "I have a big sales meeting today. I can't stay home with you. Now get ready for school."

Whenever Steve gets sick, his mother tries to stay home. But sometimes, as on this day, she can't. She does not know any baby-sitters near her home.

She gives Steve his lunch money, then runs out to her car. Steve goes to school, but by ten o'clock, he feels worse. He goes to the nurse's office. The nurse calls his mother. Her meeting will last until noon.

What do latchkey children do when they're sick? Most school and child-care centers have strict health rules. Usually, they can't keep sick children.

When children are sick, it's best that they have constant care from an adult. Parents are best. If parents must work that day, then a baby-sitter, relative, or neighbor is a good choice. It is best for children to stay in their own homes or familiar places if they are sick. If

When parents are at work, special sick-care centers help children with mild illnesses.

a sick child has to stay alone, it's a good idea for a parent to telephone home often. The child should rest, and when awake, enjoy TV, the radio, books, or other quiet activities.

Children should be taught to know when they are ill enough to call for help. The illnesses they are most likely to get and to need help with are headaches, stomachaches, vomiting, diarrhea, colds, sore throats, coughs, earaches, and fevers.

At least 55 United States cities have another choice for sick children who need care. They have special *sick-*

care centers for children with mild illnesses. Since 1987, about 80 of these have opened. Most of them are in hospitals, where nurses do most of the caretaking and doctors are on call.

Other sick-care centers, like Chicken Soup in Minneapolis, Minnesota, are not part of any hospital. Chicken Soup was the first child-care center for sick children in the United States. It and centers like it also accept children with such contagious diseases as chicken pox, and place them in separate rooms so other children won't get sick.

TenderCare for Kids, also in Minneapolis/St. Paul, Minnesota, is an in-home program for sick children. Child-care workers go to the homes of mildly sick children to care for them. TenderCare is part of Home Health Plus, a home-care agency.

SNACKS AND MEALS

After-school snacks for latchkey children are usually foods or treats that are easy to find and eat. Fruit, cookies, crackers, nuts, raisins, chips, packaged cakes and bars, candy, and yogurt are popular. Many children make peanut butter and jelly sandwiches and drink soda, milk, or fruit juices.

Many children, especially very young children, are not allowed to cook. But some help prepare meals by making salads, washing vegetables, or setting the table.

Some even make casseroles or put food into the oven to cook.

"Monday night is Dad's special meatloaf," said Bob, age thirteen. "At five, I turn on the oven. I take his meatloaf out of the refrigerator and put it in the oven. When he comes in at six, it's done!"

ALONE IN THE MORNING

Thousands of American children spend part of each weekday morning alone. The exact number or average amount of time alone is not known. What is known is that as more and more mothers work outside of the home, more and more children get themselves off to school. Some of these same children are also in self-care after school.

Some parents start their jobs at 8 or 9 A.M. Some start earlier, at 6 or 7 A.M. Factory workers, salespeople, and nurses work at different times during the day or month.

"I get sleepy by ten in the morning," said Sandy. "I wake up at five because my parents have to drop me off at my grandparents' by six. I watch TV, then catch the school bus at eight-thirty. That's a long morning for me."

Schools start at different times, too. Like Sandy's school, most schools open between 8:00 and 9:00 A.M. But some begin at 7:00 or 9:30 A.M.

Because parents' work schedules and school times

Many latchkey kids find snacks waiting for them when they come home from school. Some even start dinner so it is done when their parents get home from work.

differ, some latchkey children get up early with their parents, then watch two or three hours of television before school. These children may have to eat breakfast early, too, or miss it altogether.

Other parents take their children to school early. Some of these children have to wait outside until the doors open, even in bad weather. But many schools now let early children inside. These children may be given small classroom jobs by teachers who have come early to prepare classes. Or they may be put into the cafeteria, where they are watched by aides. Snow days can be a problem for these children, however, because parents sometimes bring them to school even though it is closed.

Unlike the slower afternoons, mornings are usually busy for latchkey children. They have to get dressed, eat breakfast, and get to school on time. "My parents and I talked about when I'd rather be on my own," explained Dan, age twelve. "I chose the morning. My alarm goes off at seven. I get up, wash, and dress. When I come downstairs, my lunch is packed and breakfast food is ready for me. I watch a little TV, then wait for the school bus by eight. Mom gets off at three, so I see her in the afternoon."

About one out of every four American children go to school with no breakfast. And many of those who do eat breakfast do not always eat well. This can be especially true for latchkey children. Because most latchkey children are not allowed to use stoves, they eat cold cereal. Or they have chips, cake, cookies, or candy bars for breakfast. Some children spend their breakfast and lunch money at fast-food restaurants. Others make their own lunches, and these may not be healthy.

Children who are alone in the morning may also miss more school. *Truancy*, or not going to school, is a national problem. In the United States, 6 to 10 percent of all school children are absent each day. School officials say the percentage is higher for latchkey children. But that has not been documented yet.

Latchkey children may miss school for several reasons. Transportation is one. If latchkey children miss a bus, they have no one to drive them to school. Even when a child gets another ride, catches a later bus, or walks to school, he or she arrives late. Teachers often want a late note. Since a morning latchkey child has no way of getting one, he or she may not go to school at all.

Not having the right note is the reason many children stay home. A child who is alone in the morning might wake up and suddenly remember "Today is the last day to bring in a signed permission slip for the field trip on Friday, and I forgot to ask Dad or Mom" or "I need a note because I was absent from school yesterday." Rather than face the teacher without the note, he or she may skip school.

Other children stay home for poorer reasons. They decide to skip school because it's nice outside, or because they haven't studied, or because they're running late. Since no parent is home to say, "Go to school," they don't.

Many children, however, keep on schedule in the morning by learning to organize the night before. They put out clothing and breakfast food, pack lunches, and refrigerate them. When they need it, they ask parents to help. They also learn to limit the number of tasks they do in the morning.

SUMMER CARE

Keeping the number of self-care hours down during the summer can be hard when parents are gone for ten or more hours each day. One popular solution is day camp. Families can often afford day camp. The problem is that camps close by three or four in the afternoon. Then latchkey children still go home to empty houses.

Spending the summer with relatives is another solution. But when they are out-of-town relatives, this can be hard, since all of the child's friends will be back home. That was the case for ten-year-old Jerry. He admitted, "I don't like going to live with my grandparents over the summer. They live in another state. I miss playing with my friends back home."

Other summer choices, like baby-sitters or day-care centers, cost a lot but take care of the problem. Then, too, many schools offer summer classes. Some children like to go to summer school; others hate it. Some children simply stay home alone.

Sheila, age thirteen, and her family combine these solutions. "I spend the first part of the summer on my own. My parents pay me to clean the house and weed the garden. In the afternoons, I shop at the mall or go to the park with my girlfriends," she said. "In August, I go to summer camp for a couple of weeks. It's fun and I like making new friends."

Most parents and children find it best to talk over all choices. Then if children are going to be on their own for any part of the day, they can plan things to do. Setting up a daily schedule is a good idea. Children can

During the summer, kids are out of school and alone the whole day. Most parents talk to their children before the summer and discuss how they will spend their days.

block off hours for doing different things like eating meals, watching TV, having free time, doing lessons, and so on.

There are many places children can go for safe fun. Some places are parks, recreation centers, playgrounds, friends' homes, and libraries. "I make up a daily list in the summer," said Sue, age ten. "Then both my parents and I know what I'll be doing. It helps me plan so I'm not bored or lonely. Besides, I don't want to watch TV all day!"

Many parents insist that all summer self-care plans include an agreement that children let parents know at all times where they are. Terry's dad calls her twice each day. Terry, age fourteen, explained, "It's nice to know Dad cares. It also keeps me responsible. I have to be where I'm supposed to be when he calls."

PROGRAMS THAT WORK

Today there are many programs for latchkey children. Day-care centers are the most common. Several are now open before and after school and during non-school days, like holidays. How the centers are run depends on what each state requires. Each day-care program has its own rules for staff, hours, transportation services, and activities. Some cost more than others. In 1987, the average cost each week for one child in a child-care program was $57. That's about $3,000 a

Day-care centers are open before and after school. Many children go there instead of going home alone.

year. The range was $50 to $120 each week per child. There are day-care nurseries for preschool children, too.

Another kind of day care is *family day-care.* Here, people in the neighborhood open their homes for children. They offer flexible hours, including evenings and weekends. As for day-care centers, rules for family day-care are different in each state. But family day-care usually costs a little less than a child-care center. In 1987, the cost ranged from $40 to $115 each week per child.

During the 1980s, *youth service agencies* added many programs for latchkey children. Some of these are Campfire Girls, Girls Clubs, Boys Clubs, YMCAs, YWCAs, Girl Scouts, Brownies, and Boy Scouts. Among the activities these offer are classes in crafts, cooking, and other useful skills.

Marcie, age twelve, found these very helpful. "I took a class in my Girl Scout troop called After-School Responsibility," she said. "I learned safety rules for when I'm on my own. Now, I always call Mom or Dad when I get home from school. If someone rings the doorbell, I look out the window. If it's someone I don't know, I don't open the door. The local fire department showed us how to handle fires. We also took first aid."

A few large businesses offer child care for their working parents. The centers are inside the company building or nearby. In 1988, although fewer than one percent of American companies had this service, many people like them.

"Each afternoon, I found it hard to do my job after three o'clock," one mother admitted. "I'd worry about my son, Tim. Day care costs too much, so nine-year-old Tim stayed alone after school. Now my company has child care right in my building. I know Tim is okay. It's easy to pick him up at the end of my work day. He's less than five minutes away!"

Some schools have extended-day programs. Children can stay at school from 6 A.M. to 6 P.M. and also during school holidays, on teacher work days, and during bad weather. These schools set up time for arts, crafts, homework, snacks, and free play. A few offer summer programs.

Parents occasionally have used libraries as unofficial after-school day-care centers. But after sitting all day at school, some children find it hard to read quietly in the library. So in 1988, several libraries started their own latchkey programs. Across America, adults and many retired people have worked with librarians to set up programs in drug education, literacy, and homework assistance for children.

There are also more than 200 telephone *hotlines* or *helplines* for children to call in the United States. People answering these phones handle more than one million calls from children each year. In large cities, the helpers speak Spanish and many other languages as well as English. The most common reason children call is because they are bored. Children also call when they are scared, feeling down, or need help settling a fight.

Ted, age thirteen, once used a hotline called Phone-Friend. "I'm alone. I think someone is trying to get into my apartment," he told them. "What should I do?" PhoneFriend began in 1982 in Pennsylvania. It was so successful that other PhoneFriend hotlines have been set up across the United States.

Another special hotline is Grandma Please, which was started in Chicago in 1984. It links older adults with latchkey children. Senior citizens take calls from 3 P.M. to 6 P.M. every day. Grandma Please hotlines have also spread to many different states.

Older adults help latchkey children in other ways as well. The National Gardening Association, for instance, has its Roots and Shoots gardens. The roots are the older people, and the shoots are the latchkey children. The two groups work together to raise vegetables and flowers. Today, more than 150 Roots and Shoots gardens exist in this country.

Hotlines and helplines were created to help any latchkey child who is feeling lonely or depressed.

Many latchkey children enjoy their time alone without their parents. They can talk with siblings, watch TV, do homework, or just relax after a day at school.

ALONE AND FEELING GOOD

"I like taking care of myself after school," said Robin, age twelve. "It's quiet when I get home. I can take my time doing my homework."

"My sisters and I divide up the chores when we come home," explained ten-year-old Bob. "We get everything done by 4:30 so we can watch our favorite TV show."

"I know how to take care of my brothers and sisters," said Dave, age thirteen. "I've learned to cook and how to handle fights. I don't mind being alone until Dad gets in at 6:00."

Like Robin, Bob, and Dave, many latchkey children like being on their own. They say, "I'm good at taking care of myself." They're also proud of the things they have learned to do for themselves and for their families. A child over eleven can do most house chores.

Some self-care families have reward systems. Following the rules and completing chores bring rewards like movies, skating, money, or shopping trips. These special rewards are often saved for the weekend. A reward like someone saying "I'm proud of you" is great every day.

Not all children like self-care. Some find it doesn't offer enough freedom. Others feel it's better than day care, which they think is for preschool and first or second graders. Heidi, a fourth grader, said, "I want to relax after a long school day. You can't do that at day care. They always want you to do something."

But many latchkey children find their time alone rewarding. They learn to cope with emergencies. They learn how to stay by themselves and organize their time. They can decide when to do their chores and homework —and they know they are helping their families.

FOR MORE INFORMATION

For more information about latchkey children, write to:

School-Age Child-Care Project
Center for Research on Women
Wellesley College
Wellesley, MA 02181

International Child Resource Institute
1810 Hopkins Street
Berkeley, CA 94707

GLOSSARY/INDEX

BABY BOOM 8—*The years between 1946 and 1958 when many American families had children.*

DAY-CARE CENTER 6, 7, 8, 34, 37, 38, 39—*A school that takes care of children. Many parents who work during the day leave their children in day-care centers.*

DORK 6—*A word for latchkey children used during the early 1900s. It soon faded from use.*

FAMILY DAY-CARE HOME 38 — *A family home where child care is given. Family day-care homes are often in nearby neighborhoods.*

GUIDELINE 13 — *A set of rules.*

HOTLINES, HELPLINES 39, 40 — *Telephone numbers to call when you need information or advice about certain subjects. There are different hotlines and helplines for different subjects.*

LATCHKEY CHILDREN 5, 6, 7, 8, 9, 11, 12, 13, 14, 15, 16, 19, 20, 21, 22, 23, 24, 27, 29, 32, 33, 34, 37, 38, 39, 40, 42, 43, 44 — *A child who regularly spends part of a day taking care of his or herself. Usually, his or her parents work during the day.*

NEGLECT 8 —*To fail to give proper care or attention.*

ONE-PARENT HOME 7, 8—*An apartment or house in which a child lives with one parent.*

SELF-CARE 8, 11, 12, 19, 21, 31, 34, 37, 43—*To care for yourself. Latchkey children regularly care for themselves during part of a day.*

GLOSSARY/INDEX

SELF-ESTEEM 9—*How you feel about yourself.*

SIBLINGS 11, 16, 17, 19, 21—*Children with the same parents.*

SICK-CARE CENTERS 28, 29—*Clinics that treat mild illnesses. Sometimes these centers are found in hospitals and other times they are in separate buildings.*

STEPBROTHER, STEPSISTER 17—*The child of a stepparent by a previous marriage.*

TRUANCY 33—*Not going to school.*

YOUTH SERVICE AGENCIES 38—*Groups that give services to young people. These include the Girl Scouts, Brownies, Boy Scouts, Campfire Girls, Girls Clubs, Boys Clubs, and so on.*